W9-DBX-762

ALLIGATORS

Tim Harris

Grolier
an imprint of
■ SCHOLASTIC

www.scholastic.com/librarypublishing

Published 2008 by Grolier
An imprint of Scholastic Library Publishing
Old Sherman Turnpike, Danbury,
Connecticut 06816

For The Brown Reference Group plc
Project Editor: Jolyon Goddard
Copy-editors: Lesley Ellis, Lisa Hughes,
   Wendy Horobin
Picture Researcher: Clare Newman
Designers: Jeni Child, Lynne Ross,
   Sarah Williams
Managing Editor: Bridget Giles

Volume ISBN-13: 978-0-7172-6215-1
Volume ISBN-10: 0-7172-6215-4

**Library of Congress
Cataloging-in-Publication Data**

Nature's children. Set 1.
   p. cm.
   Includes index.
   ISBN-13: 978-0-7172-8080-3
   ISBN-10: 0-7172-8080-2
   1. Animals--Encyclopedias, Juvenile.
   QL49.N38 2007
   590--dc22

2007018358

Printed and bound in China

PICTURE CREDITS

Front Cover: Shutterstock: Todd S. Holder.

Back Cover: Nature PL: Steven David
Miller, Peter Scoones; Shutterstock: Richard
Bowden; Superstock: Ben Manger.

Ardea: Francois Gohier 33; **Corbis**:
Charles Philip Canglalosi 29, Philip Gould
38, Michael T. Sedam 30; **Creatas**: 26–27;
FLPA: Heidi and Hans-Jurgen Kock/Minden
Pictures 20; **FLPA**: Yva Monatiuk/John
Eastcott/Minden Pictures 46; **Nature PL**:
Lynne M. Stone 12; **NHPA**: Joe Blossom 23;
Photolibrary.com: David M. Dennis 41, C.
C. Lockwood 42, 45; **Photos.com**: 2–3, 19,
34; **Shutterstock**: Frank Boelimann 7,
Tony Campbell 16, Todd S. Holder 4, 15,
J. Norman Reid 5, 11, Ian Scott 8; **Still
Pictures**: Dr. Myrna Watanabe 37.

Contents

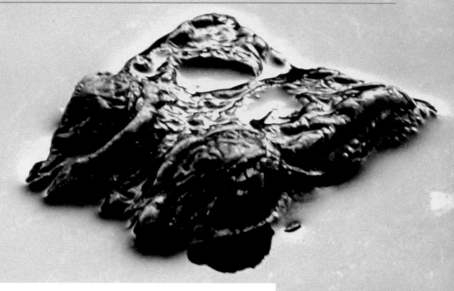

FACT FILE: Alligators

Class	Reptiles (Reptilia)
Order	Crocodilians (Crocodilia)
Family	Crocodiles (Crocodylidae)
Genus	*Alligator*
Species	American alligator (*Alligator mississippiensis*) and Chinese alligator (*Alligator sinensis*)
World distribution	The American alligator lives only in the United States; the Chinese alligator lives only in and around the Yangtze River of China
Habitat	Edges of lakes, swamps, and rivers
Distinctive physical characteristics	Black or olive green skin; short legs and a large, powerful tail; eyes, ears, and nostrils are on upper surface of the broad head
Habits	Lives alone; hibernates in burrows; female buries eggs in a mud nest and guards them
Diet	Fish, small animals, birds, and mammals

Introduction

Alligators are the kings of the swamps. These big reptiles with their tough, scaly skin and sharp teeth are great hunters, or **predators**. In their natural marshy home, no other predator would risk attacking an adult alligator. The average length of an adult alligator is 13 feet (4 m). The weight of such an alligator might vary between 490 and 590 pounds (210 and 265 kg). The biggest males grow to 19 feet (5.8 m) long.

Alligators can move around on land, but they are much more at home in water. There, alligators are excellent swimmers. They eat all kinds of animals, from tiny fish to other reptiles and even deer!

An alligator rests in mud.

What Are Alligators?

Alligators are shy animals with a fearsome reputation! They spend much of their time hidden in the water. When Spanish explorers came to the Americas hundreds of years ago, they had never seen anything like these animals. The explorers didn't know what they were. They called the alligator *el lagarto*, which means "giant lizard" in Spanish. This name is not accurate, though, because alligators are not lizards at all.

Many stories were told about alligators. One even claimed that the "giant lizards" breathed fire and smoke. That isn't true, of course. But it took a long time for scientists to discover how alligators really behave.

An alligator watches what's going on around it while most of its body is hidden underwater.

Unlike alligators, a
crocodile's teeth do
not fit together snugly.

Crocodile Cousins

Alligators and their close relatives—caimans and crocodiles—are called **crocodilians**. They are all reptiles. People often get alligators and crocodiles mixed up. That is not surprising because they look so much alike.

There are ways to tell them apart. But you need to get a good view of the animal to know for certain. Alligators and caimans have shorter, broader snouts than crocodiles. Alligators are also bigger than caimans.

There is a toothy difference between alligators and crocodiles, as well. The teeth on an alligator's lower jaw fit neatly into slots in the upper jaw when the mouth is shut. But the fourth teeth on either side of a crocodile's lower jaw don't fit snugly. They stick out when the mouth is shut.

Life in the Water

Alligators always live close to water. They prefer shallow water to deep. They would rather live in still or slow-moving water than a fast-flowing river. And they prefer freshwater to saltwater. So, the places where you are most likely to see alligators are swamps, marshes, slow-moving rivers, lakes, ponds, and canals. Sometimes, alligators live in slightly salty water, where big rivers meet the sea. But alligators never live in the open ocean.

In the swamps, alligators clear their own paths. These paths allow the alligators to travel around easily, without having to wade through dense vegetation in the water. Eventually these well-used paths widen to form creeks.

An alligator rests in the warm, marshy Florida Everglades.

The Chinese alligator
is rare and lives in only
a small area of China. It
is much smaller than its
American cousin.

Alligator Country

Alligators and their close relatives do not like cold weather. Crocodiles and caimans live only in places that are warm or hot throughout the year. But alligators can put up with colder weather. They survive spells of very cold weather, even freezing temperatures. Often, alligators dig **burrows** in the ground to keep themselves out of the cold air. Alligators need warmth for most of the year.

American alligators live in the southeastern states of the United States as well as Texas. Chinese alligators live in and around the Yangtze River of China. These places are hot in summer, but are not as warm in winter.

Armored Skin

An adult alligator's skin is olive green to black, and creamy white on the animal's underside. The skin is very tough and acts as an armor. It is thick enough to protect the alligator from attacks by other animals.

An alligator's skin is covered with rectangular **scales**. They run along the alligator's body in rows. Between the scales are narrow bands of wrinkly skin. The large scales on an alligator's back are called **scutes**. Beneath each scute is a bony plate. The scutes form ridges from the alligator's head to the tip of its tail. The scales on an alligator's belly are also tough. But they are smoother and flatter than the scutes on the reptile's back.

An alligator's skin is made up of square scales. The bumpy scales on its back are called scutes.

An alligator walks
clumsily on land.

Graceful Swimmer

Have you seen pictures of alligators sunning themselves at the edge of a swamp? The alligators look as if they don't move around very much. With their short legs, low, heavy body, and long tail, alligators are usually slow and clumsy when they walk.

Don't be fooled! If the alligator gets the chance to grab a meal, it lifts its tail off the ground and runs very quickly. But an alligator cannot move quickly on land for very long.

In the water, an alligator is a fast, graceful swimmer. Its toes have webs of skin between them. The webbing helps the alligator push itself through water. For really fast swimming, the alligator tucks its legs close to the sides of its body and swishes its powerful tail from side to side. Some male alligators swim more than 5 miles (8 km) in a day.

Underwater

There are many things about an alligator's body that help it live in water. Its eyes are high on the head and its nostrils are right at the tip of its snout. That allows the alligator to keep watch and breathe while most of its body is hidden underwater.

When the alligator is swimming underwater, it needs to protect its eyes. It also needs to keep water from entering its body through its nostrils and mouth. The eyes are protected by see-through eyelids. These special eyelids make it possible for the alligator to see when it is looking for its dinner. Muscles close the nostrils and a bony "door" at the back of the alligator's mouth shuts. This door stops water from entering the air passages and lungs. If water entered the lungs, the alligator would drown.

An alligator's nostrils (left)
poke out of the water, allowing
the reptile to breathe while
remaining mostly underwater.

An unlucky egret
becomes a meal for
a hungry alligator.

Ambush!

Some predators move around when they are looking for a meal. But not alligators. They usually stay in one place. They wait for **prey** to come close to them and then they attack. Animals that hunt in this way are called **ambush predators**.

An ambushing alligator keeps very still. It is often hidden in the water. The alligator's dark, bumpy skin looks a bit like the bark of a tree floating in the water. Many animals do not take any notice—until it's too late!

If prey is not close enough to grab, an alligator moves slowly closer and closer. When the victim is close enough, the alligator rushes forward. The alligator makes a grab, snapping its jaws around the prey. A small animal usually dies immediately or is swallowed whole. A larger animal might put up a fight. Then, the alligator tries to pull the prey underwater and hold it there until it drowns.

Teeth

An alligator's jaws and teeth are just right for catching and holding large prey. Very powerful muscles shut the jaws tight. The jaws are lined with large, sharp, cone-shaped teeth. There are about 40 teeth in the upper jaw and the same number in the lower jaw. Each tooth is hollow. When a tooth is worn out, it is pushed out of the mouth by a new tooth growing underneath.

The teeth bite into the flesh of any animal the alligator catches. They are good at keeping hold of the meal. But the teeth are not very good at chewing. Fortunately, that does not matter because the alligator usually swallows its food whole. If the prey is too large, the alligator uses its huge, strong jaws to tear it into chunks that are small enough to swallow.

Chinese alligators have flatter teeth than their American cousins. Flatter teeth are better for crushing the shells of snails and mussels than for tearing off chunks of meat. Not surprisingly, crushing shells is exactly what these teeth are used for!

A Chinese alligator
has flatter teeth than
its American cousin.

23

Lazy 'Gators

Although alligators are big, they don't use up energy very quickly. They do not need to eat as often as you might think. Sometimes, an alligator catches a tasty meal but doesn't bother to swallow it for hours!

Sometimes alligators are too lazy to catch living fish and mammals. These alligators prefer to eat **carrion**, which is animals that have already died.

In addition to dead and live animals, alligators also swallow pebbles and other hard objects. The alligator does not get any nutrients from these things. It eats them to help break up the large pieces of meat in its stomach. The pebbles make the meat easier to digest, or break down.

Territory

In the Florida Everglades, you might hear a loud bellowing sound coming from a swamp. This sound is most likely an alligator telling the world to keep out of its **territory**. Its territory is an area of water and land the alligator has claimed for itself. When threatened, the "owner" of the territory closes its mouth and forces air out of its nostrils to make a loud noise. That is the alligator's way of saying: "Get out! This place is already taken!"

Adult male alligators have a territory that other adult males are not allowed to enter. What happens then if another male wanders in? The males might fight, but that does not happen often. More likely, the owner of the territory charges toward the newcomer, hissing loudly. This scary show usually works. The unwelcome visitor leaves without either alligator getting hurt.

Alligators have about 80 sharp teeth!

Keeping Cool

Our body temperature, and that of other mammals, remains pretty much the same whatever the weather. A human's temperature is always around 98.6°F (37°C). That is why mammals are described as "**warm-blooded**."

Alligators and other reptiles are not warm-blooded. Their body temperature goes up and down as the weather changes. On a scorching summer's day, alligators can get too hot. To cool off, they might rest in the shade of a big tree or wallow in the shallow water of a swamp. They can also cool down by opening their jaws to let heat escape through the damp lining of their mouth.

On a cool night or in winter, alligators have a different problem: they can get so cold that their muscles do not work. These "**cold-blooded**" animals have found some interesting ways to keep warm when the weather gets cold.

An alligator opens its mouth to cool down.

An alligator begins
burrowing in mud.

Staying Warm

When the weather gets chilly, so does an alligator's body. Most alligators live in places that are warm all year. But some alligators live in parts of the United States that can get cold in winter. To stay warm during these cold spells, alligators burrow into the soft mud of a riverbank. They might also make a shelter among the roots of a big tree.

Chinese alligators have to protect themselves from the winter cold, too. They dig underground burrows. Sometimes, they stay in a state of inactivity, or **dormant**, for several months in winter. Because these alligators are not active in winter, they use very little energy. Therefore, they do not need to eat in winter. When the weather gets warmer, they come out again— and hunt for a meal!

'Gator Holes

Dry and hot weather can make life difficult for alligators. Most of the prey they eat either live in water or visit water to drink. So if the water dries up, the alligator might go hungry.

But alligators do not let that stop them. When the level of water in their swamp or river gets too low, alligators swish their tail and wiggle their body on the muddy bottom. The remaining water pools in these 'gator-made depressions, or deeper areas. These deeper areas are called "gator holes." Even when the shallow water has dried up, the 'gator holes stay wet.

In their own search for water, fish and other water animals end up in the 'gator hole as well. So the alligator does not have to move far to find its dinner!

An alligator swishes its tail and body from side to side to make a 'gator hole.

A male and female American alligator prepare to mate.

A Noisy Courtship

The **mating season** for American alligators is usually in April and May. Swamps become much noisier at this time, as male and female alligators pair up. Male alligators growl and bellow so loudly they can be heard for miles. Female alligators interested in mating swim toward the source of noise. When a male and female alligator see each other they sometimes lift their head above the water and splash it down very hard. That is called "head-slapping," and alligators are very good at it!

The real courtship then takes place, usually in the water. The alligators rub each other's back and snout. The male might even blow bubbles across the female's snout. If the female likes the male, she lets him climb on her back and mate with her.

Nesting

After a pair of alligators has mated, the male goes away. It is the female who then does all the hard work. She first has to build a nest. The nest has to be close to water so she can get to it easily. It also has to be a little bit higher than the water level in case there is a flood. If her eggs are covered with water, the eggs will not hatch. The nest must be shaded from bright sunshine, too. A female often builds a nest in the shade of trees or bushes.

When she has chosen a spot, the female alligator builds a large mound of mud, leaves, and other plant material. She makes a little hole on top of the mound. She lays her eggs in the hole. Then she covers the eggs with soil.

A female alligator makes a hole in her nest where she will lay her eggs.

Alligator eggs sit
snugly in their nest.

Guard Duty

American alligators usually lay between 40 and 45 eggs. But a full-grown alligator may lay as many as 50 eggs. Alligator eggs are bright white and almost twice the size of a chicken's egg. Alligator eggs make a tasty meal for a hungry raccoon or snake. The mother alligator must guard them carefully until they hatch.

It's a long wait. The eggs will not hatch for about two months. During this time, the baby alligators inside grow slowly. They feed on the yolk of the egg. If for any reason the eggs get too cold, the baby alligators die. Usually, though, the eggs stay nice and warm in their nest. The time from when the eggs are laid to when they hatch is called the **incubation period**.

If a hungry animal tries to get at the eggs in the nest, the mother hisses and lunges at the intruder. Usually, she scares away the visitor without having to fight. After all, she does look and sound very scary!

Hatchlings

Baby alligators are ready to hatch about 65 days after the eggs are laid. But how do they get out of their egg? The babies have a hard bump on the end of their snout called an **egg tooth**. They use the egg tooth to carve a way out of the hard eggshell. The egg tooth drops off a few days after the young alligators hatch.

Once out of the egg, the hatchlings grunt so their mother knows they are ready for life in the outside world. She opens the nest mound with her jaws and front legs, and out come her babies! They look like tiny versions of their parents and are only about 9 inches (22 cm) long. That is about the length of a new pencil.

A baby alligator
breaks out of
its egg.

41

Young alligators hang out together in a 'gator hole in Louisiana.

Boys or Girls?

If an alligator lays 40 eggs, how many will be male and how many will be female? You might guess that half would be male and half female. Often, however, all the eggs in a nest turn out to be male. Or all might be female.

It is the temperature that actually affects whether the young are male or female. If the eggs were incubated in a cool nest, the young turn out to be male. If the eggs developed in a warmer nest, the young turn out to be female.

A hatchling can see and move around as soon as it comes out of its egg. It has two tiny jaws, four little legs, and a tiny tail. The belly sticks out because it is full of leftover yolk. The baby still feeds on this yolk for its first few days. The youngster's belly is dirty white. It becomes yellow within a week and darkens as the alligator gets older.

Dangerous Times

After leaving the nest, the hatchlings make their way to the water. They are safer there than they are on land. But they still face many dangers. The baby alligators are lucky because their mother tries to watch over them as they grow. She cannot see every danger, though, especially when there are so many youngsters to care for. Large fish, snapping turtles, herons, and bullfrogs will snap up the babies if given a chance. About nine out of every ten babies die before they reach their first birthday.

The young alligators stay together all winter in groups called pods. In the first year of the young alligators' life, their mother protects them. She rushes to help if she hears one of them squeal. Most of the time, though, the small alligators take care of themselves. The babies find their own shelter and hunt tadpoles, crayfish, and bugs.

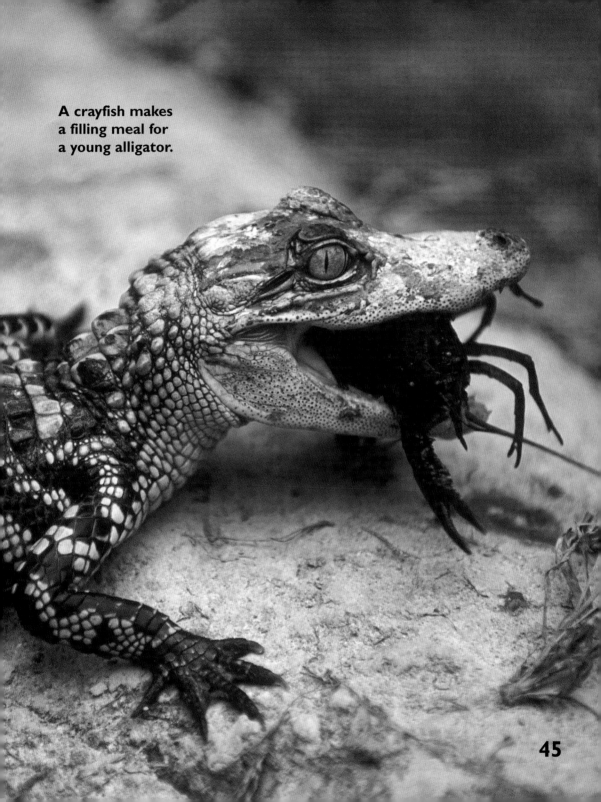

A crayfish makes
a filling meal for
a young alligator.

American alligators
have silvery eyes.

Growing Up

When an alligator is a year old, it might be more than 2 feet (60 cm) long. That's big enough to look after itself. Young alligators might stay close to where they hatched for up to three years. After that, the mother chases them away. If she didn't do that, there would be too many alligators in a small area. There wouldn't be enough food for all of them.

The young alligators must find their own territory. That can be difficult. A young alligator looks for a part of the swamp with lots of fish, frogs, and other good things to eat. There, the alligator can grow quickly. But if the youngster's territory does not have much food, the alligator grows more slowly.

A Long Life

Alligators grow quickly until they are about
9 feet (2.7 m) long. Then, they grow more
slowly. Some males do not stop growing until
they are 16 feet (5 m) long. Measure this length
out on your kitchen floor and you'll see just
how long an alligator can be!

Male American alligators are old enough
to mate when they are about five years old.
By this time they have reached a length of
about 6 feet (2 m). Female alligators grow more
slowly. They are ready to mate when they are
about 10 years old and 6 feet (2 m) long.

As an alligator grows, its tough outer skin is
shed in tiny flakes. New skin grows underneath
the old. New teeth grow, too, when old teeth
wear out.

If an alligator survives its dangerous
childhood, it will be bigger than its enemies.
The alligator will probably live a long life and
raise many of its own children. In the wild,
alligators tend to live between 35 and 50 years.

Words to know

Ambush predators   Animals that lie in wait for their prey.

Burrows   Holes in the ground dug by an animal and used as a home.

Carrion   The rotting flesh of dead animals.

Cold-blooded   Term used for animals that have no internal control of their body temperature.

Crocodilians   The group of reptiles that includes alligators, crocodiles, and caimans.

Dormant   In a sleeplike state in which an animal does not move or feed.

Egg tooth   A hard point on a baby reptile's nose that it uses to break out of its shell.

49

Incubation period	The time between eggs being laid and their hatching.
Mating season	Time of the year when animals come together to produce young.
Predators	Animals that hunt other animals.
Prey	An animal that is hunted as food by other animals (predators).
Scales	Thin, hard plates that cover an alligator's skin.
Scutes	Large bumpy scales on an alligator's back.
Territory	Area that an animal lives in and defends from other animals.
Warm -blooded	Term used for animals that have internal control of their body temperature. Birds and mammals are warm-blooded.

Find Out More

Books

Dennard, D. *Reptiles: Explore the Fascinating Worlds Of Alligators and Crocodiles, Lizards, Snakes, Turtles.* Our Wild World. Minnetonka, Minnesota: Northword Press, 2004.

Richardson, A. *Alligators.* Bridgestone Books World of Reptiles. Mankato, Minnesota: Bridgestone Books, 2005.

Web sites

Alligator
www.enchantedlearning.com/subjects/reptiles/alligator/coloring.shtml
Information about and a diagram of an alligator.

Fun Facts About: Alligators
www.cclockwood.com/gatorcam/kidspage.htm
Interesting facts about alligators.

Index